Holiness of the Heart

HOLINESS OF THE HEART

"The heart that pleases the Lord and brings the Father joy"
"Guard your heart above all else,
for it determines the course of your life"

(Proverbs 4:23; NLT)

Princess Wesay

ReadersMagnet, LLC

Holiness of the Heart
Copyright © 2022 by *Princess Wesay*

Published in the United States of America
ISBN   Paperback: 978-1-957312-70-5
ISBN   eBook: 978-1-957312-71-2

All rights reserved. No part of this publication may be reproduced, stored in a retrieval system or transmitted in any way by any means, electronic, mechanical, photocopy, recording or otherwise without the prior permission of the author except as provided by USA copyright law.

The opinions expressed by the author are not necessarily those of ReadersMagnet, LLC.

ReadersMagnet, LLC
10620 Treena Street, Suite 230 | San Diego, California, 92131 USA
1.619. 354. 2643 | www.readersmagnet.com

Book design copyright © 2022 by ReadersMagnet, LLC. All rights reserved.

Cover design by *Ericka Obando*
Interior design by *Dorothy Lee*

TABLE OF CONTENTS

Introduction 9

CHAPTER ONE

Why the heart? 11
Crucial to life 11
Man cannot see it 12
It is deceitful 13
God sees it 13
You know what's in it 15
You can change it 16

CHAPTER TWO

Type of Hearts 17
Bad Heart 18
Example 18
Evil Heart 19
Deceitful Heart 20
Unrepentant Heart 21
Selfish Heart 22
Unbelieving Heart 22
Doubtful Heart 23
A Trouble Heart 24
Jealous Heart 25
Bitter heart 25
Broken Heart 27
A Wounded Heart 27

Hearts that pleases the Lord 28
A Good Heart 28
Pure heart 28
A God-fearing heart 29
A Contrite Heart 29
A Truthful Heart 30
Trustful Heart 30
Loving Heart 31
A Caring Heart 32

CHAPTER THREE

Caring for the Heart 33
Examine your heart daily 34
Check your motives 35
Pray for a clean heart daily 36
Don't harbor evil in your heart 37
Don't dwell on evil 37
Don't dwell on the bad behaviors of people 38
Dwell on good things 39
Dwell on pure thoughts 39
Owned Your heart 41

CHAPTER FOUR

Come to God 42
Receive God's rest 43
Lean on His promises 44

CHAPTER FIVE

Rewards of the Hearts 45
Results of a wrong heart 45
Your Understanding is darkened 45
Spiritual Cancer 46

Unworthy to make heaven.. 46
Unable to breakthrough.. 47
People will stay away from you 47
Rewards of a Good Heart.. 48
You will see God 48
God will be good to you.. 48
You are qualified to stand before God... 49
You will attract good people 49
You will receive your heart desires 50
Pure Heart and Prayer... 50

Conclusion... 51

INTRODUCTION

The issue of our hearts is very significant to God, ourselves, and others. This is so important that whenever it is spoken about in scripture the writer uses the word above. The word above means higher or on the top. It also means superior. When something or someone is above that means that thing or person is significant and one can not do without or go further without that thing or person being involved or affected. There are also 1400 verses on the heart and spirit in scripture. This tells me that the heart needs attention. The heart is that one area that we need to closely pay attention to if we want to enjoy our walk with God, have a good relationship with others, fulfilling our purpose, and making it to heaven. The issue of the heart has become personal to me on many occasions in my walk with God. When I discovered how important it is to my personal relationship with God, my success in life, as an intercessor, and as a pastor I began to take it very seriously. Before I was instructed to write this book I always paid keen attention to my heart when praying, preaching, and leading others in prayer. It becomes even more personal to me especially when I am dealing with difficult people and handling conflict. In my second book "Forgiveness is for you and a must if you want to enjoy your Christian life and make heaven" I discuss the condition of our hearts when we don't forgive. I always emphasize the importance of our hearts being clean every time I lead prayer until one day I did a teaching on it and that teaching by the power of the Holy Spirit truly set many people free. I was then led by the Holy Spirit to write this book. On April 11, 2021, I was led to read about an encounter of a great WOG Anna Rountree, in this encounter she explained and was told by our Lord Jesus that the following things bring God joy and please him. The following are Obedience, Holiness of Heart, Thankfulness, and Truth with mercy. When I learned that Holiness of the Heart brings God Joy I was deeply moved and had the confirmation that this book is a must and urgently needed in the body of Christ. The next morning while spending time with the Lord, as I was writing in my journey the Lord begin to speak to me that I needed to finish up my second book and write this book before the fall of 2021. He said both books should be out by this time. With this instruction and in obedience to the Lord I decided to write these books as quickly as possible. I believe many of us have missed a lot of blessings and this causes God to be saddened because of the conditions of our hearts. It is my prayer as you read this book it will not be another piece of information but instead you will cultivate and have Holiness of Heart. May the good Lord who delights in a pure heart impart unto you as you yield and surrender your heart to him. Receive it now in the name of Jesus.

CHAPTER ONE
Why the heart?

The heart needs attention because of the following: It is crucial to life, Man cannot see it, it is deceitful, God sees it, you know what's in it, and you can change it.

CRUCIAL TO LIFE

As it is said, Spiritual things are sometimes parallel to physical things. Jesus our Lord understood this principle very well that is why he always used parables to teach. He used what the people were familiar with, to present his message. The same is true today. If we understand things in the natural realm or physical. We can easily understand spiritual things. Nevertheless, Life is more spiritual than physical so having a true understanding of the spiritual realm is even better. Why the heart? The heart is one of the most significant parts of the human body. It circulates blood and provides the body with the oxygen and nutrients it needs to survive. Without blood, humans will be unable to fight infection and survive. Once the heart stops pumping blood and when there's no heartbeat that person's life is at the crucial stage and when help is not given quickly they are considered dead. Just as the human heart is that crucial to the survival of a person it is also crucial to one's spiritual life. It is also one of the most important parts of our spiritual life. Without a good spiritual heart, a person's spiritual life is in jeopardy and can lead that one to spiritual death and if care is not taken that person can end up in hell.

> *"For out of the heart come evil thoughts, murder, adultery, sexual immorality, theft, false testimony, slander"*
>
> *(Matthew 15:19; NIV).*

The heart is indeed crucial to our life because out of it flows good and evil. The scripture above shows what the heart produces when care is not taken.

Man cannot see it

"Who really knows how bad it is?"(Jeremiah 17:9b).

Another reason why one needs to pay attention to his or her heart is because man cannot see inside one's heart except God and that person. Man is not only unable to see the heart but the scripture above describes the condition of the heart and how bad the heart is. If something is considered bad, wouldn't you want to pay attention to it? I do and believe God wants us to, that's why you are reading this book. Since man is unable to see our hearts it is easy to pretend to be something you are not because no one sees what's inside. For example. you can pretend on the outward that you have forgiven someone and many will think you really did but inside your heart, you have not forgiven that person. One can also pretend to love someone that they truly hate and no one will know because their outward actions may be good but inward is bad. The scripture says who really knows how bad the heart is, we, therefore, need to pay attention to the heart and care for it as we would care for our physical heart.

IT IS DECEITFUL

"The heart is deceitful above all things and beyond cure. Who can understand it?"Jeremiah 17:9;NIV).

The third reason why the heart needs attention is that it is deceitful and beyond cure says the Lord. When something is deceitful it is considered misleading or untruthful. As we know a misleading or untruthful situation or information can be detrimental to one's life and the lives of others. A misleading heart will cause one to live in continuous deception. The heart is not only considered deceitful, it is also beyond cure. When something is beyond cure, it needs constant attention and care to survive. Our heart, therefore, needs that daily care and attention to survive. This constant care and attention will help us have a healthy relationship with God and will keep us on the road to heaven.

GOD SEES IT

"But the Lord said to Samuel, "Do not look at his appearance or his physical stature, because I have refused him. For *the Lord does* not *see* as man sees; for man looks at the outward appearance, but the Lord looks at the heart."(1 Samuel 16:7;NKJV).

The fourth reason why the heart needs careful attention is God sees it and makes his judgment from there. As we know having a good and healthy relationship with God is not only important but it helps one to become everything God has for them and all the tools needed to fulfill his or her purpose. Nothing is hidden from God, we can never hide from his presence. He knows what is in our heart therefore

He cannot be deceived. With this knowledge, one heart is seen by God and if you want to have a good relationship with him you will have to care daily for your heart. As the scriptures say he looks at our hearts when deeding with us and making his judgments. By our hearts, we can either be accepted by God or rejected. The story with David and his brothers is a perfect example. God knew the hearts of David's brothers and knew they were not qualified by his standard to take over the kingdom from Saul. He knew that David truly loved him and was a man after his heart that is why he chose David above his brothers.

Our hearts can determine our promotion and lifting by God. Our hearts can help God decide who to use when there's a need that requires his intervention.

Care for your heart and it will do you good. Our hearts can determine our promotion and lifting by God.

You know what's in it

"Your word I have hidden in my heart, That I might not sin against You"

(Psalms 119:11).

The fifth reason we need to pay attention to our heart is we know what's in it. What is hidden in your hearts? What are you keeping in your heart? Is it good or evil? It is righteousness or unrighteous? The above scripture can help us determine whether our hearts are filled with goodness or evil. One can deceive himself or herself by ignoring the reality of what they are dealing with. If you are bitter and carrying unforgiveness, you know it. No man may see it because it is within you, you may pretend but deep within your heart, you know the battle you are facing or the heaviness you are dealing with due to, malice, hatred, bitterness, and unforgiveness. Since we know what's in our heart we can decide to fix it and present ourselves to God. We are also able to humble ourselves before the Lord and ask him for help. If we decide not to ask others for prayer because one is ashamed, God can help that person if he or she is sincere by confessing his or her sin and asking God for help. Don't ignore what's in your heart if you know what is in it is evil, please don't pretend by saying it's okay, Take care of your heart if it's damage by paying keen attention to it. This takes us to the next reason why we need to care for our hearts.

You can change it

*"Create in me a clean heart, O God,
And renew a steadfast spirit within me"*

(Psalms 51:10).

The sixth reason why we need to care for our hearts is we can change it if evil is abiding in it. One has the ability to change whatever they don't need in their life. You have the power to change what's in your personal life especially when it comes to your inner man or spiritual life. Just as we can pray and ask God for material things we can do the same with inner issues such as the condition of our hearts. One thing that is constant with God as we all know is holiness. Holiness is the very air he breathes. God cannot be separated from holiness. As his children, we have to deal with him on this level. So, if you know that your heart is full of evil you can boldly confess those evil and ask the Lord to change your heart. Like David said in the above scripture, Lord create in me a clean heart. David recognized the condition of his heart and repented of his sins and asked the Lord for a clean heart. The same is yours if you ask the Lord today for a change of heart. Receive it as you have asked in the name of Jesus.

CHAPTER TWO
Type of Hearts

As I begin to discuss the types of hearts I will break them into two Categories. The first category is called the wrong heart and the second is called the right heart. When the Heart goes wrong or is wrong, everything in your life will go wrong, a wrong heart affects the issues of your life. A wrong heart will prevent you from making heaven and will also hinder the blessings of God in your life. A wrong heart consists of the following: Bad heart, deceitful heart, unrepentant heart, wounded heart, selfish heart, unbelieving heart, doubtful heart, evil heart, trouble heart, jealous heart, bitter heart, and a broken heart. The second category consists of, good heart, A pure heart, a God-fearing heart, a contrite heart, a truthful heart, a trustful heart, a loving heart, and a caring heart. The first category of the heart is the most dangerous and God wants us to stay away from it. The second category is called a right heart, when the heart is right everything falls in place and this is the kind of heart the Lord wants us to cultivate. Let's go through the first category and be free in the name of Jesus.

Hearts that God hates

Bad Heart

"For out of the heart come evil thoughts—murder, adultery, sexual immorality, theft, false testimony, slander"(Matthew 15:19"

A bad heart is defined as an unpleasant or unfortunate heart. It is an unwelcoming heart. This heart produces evil thoughts. It is where the desire to murder, steal, commits adultery, fornicate, sexual immorality, slanderous and false witnesses comes from. This heart is very dangerous, nothing good comes from it. All of its desire is nothing but everything that God and his word oppose. It produces unfruitful desires. This heart is considered destructive and it is the kind of heart Satan and his kingdom operate from. This heart proceeds from darkness and is sustained by the dark powers of this world. When the religious leader questioned Jesus about the washing of hands as it relates to their tradition of purity, Jesus quickly rebuked them by saying it was not what one eats or what goes in the heart, it is what proceeds from it. He says one is defiled by what is in their heart. A bad heart is just that.

Example

An example of someone with a bad heart is someone who doesn't want anything good for anyone. This person's intentions towards people are bad, whenever this person does something for someone or have an opportunity to be around people they will make sure their victims are destroyed. This person is controlled by a demon and works for Satan directly or indirectly.

Evil Heart

"But they did not listen or pay attention; instead, they followed the stubborn inclinations of their evil hearts. They went backward and not forward"
(Jeremiah 7:24;NIV).

An evil heart is a heart that has no good in it. It is the absence of good. All that is in this heart is nothing but evil. This kind of heart is a good example of the dark world. It is the kind of heart that the devil desires of people so he can effectively use them. I heard this testimony and confession of a devil worshipper, she said the devil looks for people who have kind hearts to use them to accomplish his purpose. She said kind-hearted people when they get converted to satanism they are eviler than anyone else. An evil-hearted person will go to any extreme to damage the lives of others. Nothing good proceeds from this heart. Every thought and action of this person is evil and destruction. As the scripture says this person will not listen because of the pride and stubbornness of his or her heart. They would prefer going backward in life by opposing everything that is good. This kind of heart is not of the Lord and cannot be tolerated in the kingdom of God. This is the reason why when we come to the Lord in salvation he changes our heart and gave us a new heart that will accept his teachings and follow his path.

Deceitful Heart

"The heart is deceitful above all things, and beyond cure. Who can understand it?"

Jeremiah 17:9

A deceitful heart is a misleading heart. It is a heart filled with lies or false impressions. As the scripture says above it is beyond cure. It is a kind of heart that glories satan. As you may know, if you are familiar with the deeds of satan, he is a deceiver and loves to keep people in deception. This kind of heart will make you live life for the devil and will take you to hell if you don't repent. A deceitful heart will also keep you in bondage. It makes you live a pretentious life, for example, you know you have issues or need help with some areas of your life but this kind of heart will tell you that you are fine. This is just you and you don't need to do anything with your behaviors or actions. A deceitful heart will also keep others in bondage, for example, a guy or lady who has a deceitful heart will date two or more persons at the same time and lie to each of them promising to marry them. This kind of heart is so deceitful that if care is not taken it creates trauma for the victim and they can live with regrets all the days of their life. Indeed, who can understand it? It is dangerous. Please stay away from such heart.

Unrepentant Heart

"But because of your stubbornness and your unrepentant heart, you are storing up wrath against yourself for the day of God's wrath, when his righteous judgment will be revealed"

(Romans 2:5;NIV).

An unrepentant heart is a heart that shows no regret for one's wrongdoings. It is an unapologetic heart. A person with such a heart doesn't see anything wrong with their actions or lifestyle. This person's heart is filled with stubbornness and pride. This person knows they have sinned but refuses to repent or ask forgiveness. This person also enjoys their lifestyle even though it is unnatural for what they do but because of stubbornness, they will not repent. The enemy keeps such a person in darkness and he or she never recognizes his or her need for help. As the scripture says, you are storing up wrath against your own soul. You will be judged for not repenting and refusing the opportunities that were given to you to repent and for ignoring your conscience and not repenting. May this not be your portion in the name of Jesus. If you are currently in this state please repent by praying the salvation pray in the beginning or back of the book. Receive grace now as you do.

SELFISH HEART

"For all seek their own, not the things which are of Christ Jesus"(Philippians 2:21;NKJV).

"*Let* nothing *be done* through selfish ambition or conceit, but in lowliness of mind let each esteem others better than himself" (Philippians 2:3;NKJV).

A Selfish heart is a heart that lacks consideration for others, people with such heart are chiefly concerned about their profit or pleasure. It becomes all about them. They have no regard for the needs of others or the feelings of other people. They always seek their benefit. They seek not the things of Christ or what brings the Lord glory. Life is center on them. Their ambitions are always selfish. They seek great things for their pleasure. They are full of themselves. May this don't be your portion in the name of Jesus.

UNBELIEVING HEART

See to it, brothers and sisters, that none of you has a sinful, unbelieving heart that turns away from the living God"(Hebrews 3:12; NIV).

An unbelieving heart is a heart that doesn't believe or a heart that has no faith. It is a heart of disbelief. People with such hearts may experience or have knowledge of God but yet still refuse to believe what God has done or is doing. An example of this can be seen throughout the book of Exodus as it relates to the children of Israel, these people saw real miracles, they saw and experienced the mighty hand of God but chose to still walk in unbelief. As the result of their unbelief, God says they will not enter his rest. Some did not enter the promised land. This kind of heart will make you missed heaven. As the scripture says it is a sinful heart that turns away from God. Sometimes people that have an unbelieving heart turn to other gods that are unable to save them. Some become worshippers of idols because until they physically see something they wouldn't believe it. An unbelieving heart is a heart that is not pleasing to God and doesn't bring God's glory and it is an impure heart.

DOUBTFUL HEART

"Have faith in God," Jesus answered. "Truly I tell you, if anyone says to this mountain, 'Go, throw yourself into the sea,' and does not doubt in their heart but believes that what they say will happen, it will be done for them. Therefore I tell you, whatever you ask for in prayer, believe that you have received it, and it will be yours"(Mark 11:22-24;NIV)

A doubtful heart is a heart of uncertainty or a heart that lacks true conviction. This kind of heart does not only prevent you from going to heaven but it also hinders the blessings of God in your life. The Bible teaches us to believe without doubting as the scripture says from Jesus' very mouth if we ask anything of the father when we pray and we don't doubt in our hearts it shall be given unto us. As a servant of God, I have come across believers who continue to doubt God and because of this, their blessings are hindered. If you are currently experiencing doubts in your life. I set you free now in the name of Jesus. A doubtful heart is also a heart that lacks trust in the Lord. It is very important to know and understand if we claim to know God and don't trust him or his unadulterated word we are losing out. In Hebrew 11:6 The scripture tells us that if we come to God we must believe that first of all God exists and he is a rewarder of those that diligently seek him. If you know he exists please believe that he rewards those that trust him with all of their hearts and have no doubt about his existence and working on the earth. "And without faith it is impossible to please God because anyone who comes to him must believe that he exists and that he rewards those who earnestly seek him"(Hebrews 11:6;NIV).

A Trouble Heart

"Do not let your hearts be troubled. You believe in God; believe also in me"(John 14:1;NIV).

A troubled heart is a heart of disturbance or a disorderly heart. This heart is out of order due to worries and other concerns of this world. Jesus encourages us to stay away from such hearts because it can be detrimental to our health and happiness. A heart that is troubled will not make good decisions. People with such a heart always find themselves in negative circles. This heart can also be seen as a heart that lacks faith and trust in the Lord. This is the reason why Jesus says believe in God and also believe in me because he knew lack of faith would be a serious problem with troubled hearts.

Jealous Heart

"But if you have bitter jealousy and selfish ambition in your heart, do not be arrogant and so lie against the truth. This wisdom is not that which comes down from above but is earthly, natural, demonic. For where jealousy and selfish ambition exist, there is disorder and every evil thing"
(James 3:14-16;NASB).

A Jealous heart is a disorderly heart. It is a heart that shows feelings or envy of someone else's achievements, successes, and blessings. This heart is never satisfied with what it has, it always wants or wishes what others have. It is always eyeing others' blessings and success. It is a heart that is filled with insecurities. This heart can easily end up in demonic activities because of its selfish longings. Its ambition is all about this world. It is filled with evil and envy. It is a distrustful and suspicious heart. Its end is destruction because it lacks the truth and wisdom of God.

Bitter heart

*"Each heart knows its bitterness,
and no one else can share its joy"*

(Proverbs 14:10;NIV).

A Bitter heart is a heart that lacks joy. It is a heart that holds a grudge and refuses to forgive. It is a heart that has a strong resentment against someone. A bitter heart or a person with a bitter heart has a strong tendency of justifying their bitterness. A person with a bitter heart is always angry, demands control because of hurts and insecurity. They are also always grumpy, moody, unhappy, and become annoyed when you try to talk about the issue. A bitter heart is the result of hurts, disappointments, letdowns, and betrayals. A bitter heart is very unhealthy because it is filled with pain and steals the joy and peace of the one who is bitter. The following are some consequences of a person with a bitter heart.

1. A bitter heart makes you defile or unworthy to stand before the Lord...

> *"See to it that no one falls short of the grace of God and that no bitter root grows up to cause trouble and defile many"*
> *(Hebrews 12:15;NIV).*

2. A bitter heart can develop into an evil heart....

> *"For I see that you are in the gall of bitterness and the bond of iniquity"*
> *(Acts 8:23;ESV).*

3. A bitter heart stops and steals your prosperity.....

> *"Another dies in bitterness of soul, never having tasted of prosperity"*
> *(Job 21:25;ESV).*

4. A bitter heart leads you to destruction....

> *"Behold, it was for my welfare that I had great bitterness, but in love you have delivered my life from the pit of destruction, for you have cast all of my sins behind your back"*
> *(Isaiah 38:17;ESV).*

5. ..A Bitter heart slows down your life......

BROKEN HEART

"My flesh and my heart may fail, but God is the strength of my heart and my portion forever"
Psalms 73:26

A broken heart is a heart that has experienced failure and extreme hurts. It is also a heart that is grief as the result of the loss. It is a sad heart. This kind of heart can only be healed by God. God is near to anyone who has a broken heart. He is the answer and healer of the broken. The Psalm encourages us that God will strengthen the brokenhearted. If you are currently experiencing or have a broken heart, receive healing now in the name of Jesus.

A WOUNDED HEART

"He heals the brokenhearted and binds up their wounds"

(Psalms 147:3, NIV).

A Wounded heart is a heart that suffers injury or extreme hurts that is unbearable due to overpowering negative emotions as a result of disappointments, betrayals, lies, false accusations, etc. A wounded heart tends to become bitter and hateful because of the pains and disappointments. A person will a wounded heart can not pray effectively until he or she truly forgives their offender. As Cindy Jacobs puts it" A wounded heart cannot be entrusted with God's secrets because it does not pray with pure motive". A wounded heart is a hurting heart and people with such hearts have a payback attitude to satisfy that pain. They want their offenders to pay for their sins.

Hearts that pleases the Lord

The second category of the heart is a heart that pleases the Lord. Let's go through them and be imparted in the name of Jesus.

A Good Heart

"A good man brings good things out of the good stored up in his heart, and an evil man brings evil things out of the evil stored up in his heart. For the mouth speaks what the heart is full of"
(Luke 6:45;NIV).

A good heart is a heart that is stored with good intentions and produces good fruits. This is a God-kind of heart. In this heart proceeds no evil, all it desires is good and the wellbeing of others. It is a selfless heart. It looks out for others and follows the mind of God.

Pure heart

"Blessed are the pure in heart, for they will see God"
(Matthew 5:8;NIV).

A pure heart is a heart without malice or evil intent, it is an honest, sincere, and guileless heart. A Person with a pure heart as the scriptures say will see God. They can easily connect with God because there is no hindrance. This heart is priceless and is to be desired by everyone who wants to see God and make heaven.

A God-fearing heart

"To fear the Lord is to hate evil; I hate pride and arrogance, evil behavior and perverse speech"

(Proverbs 8:13;NIV).

A God-fearing heart is a heart that hates all evil and clings to righteousness and that which is lovely and pure. This heart fears the Lord in all things. This heart truly honors God. It will not entertain evil nor participate in it. A person with a God-fearing heart always thinks about the integrity of God when he or she is making an everyday decision.

A Contrite Heart

"My hands have made both heaven and earth; they and everything in them are mines.

I, the Lord, have spoken! "I will bless those who have humble and contrite hearts, who tremble at my word"
(Isaiah 66:2;NLT).

A contrite heart is a remorseful and repentant heart. When you have a contrite heart you don't enjoy wrong or enjoy sinning. You don't find pleasure in sinning, you have this deep kind of sorrow within your heart when you sin. A person with a contrite heart has no desire to sin because of their love and fear of God. They are easily broken and ready to always do right. A Person with a contrite heart doesn't wait for a preacher to tell them their wrong before he or she repents. They immediately change when they wrong God and others. As the scripture says this person is humble and trembles at the word of God. Receive this heart now in the name of Jesus.

A Truthful Heart

"Let us draw near with a true heart in full assurance of faith, having our hearts sprinkled from an evil conscience and our bodies washed with pure water"
(Hebrews 10:22;NKJV)

A truthful heart is an honest heart. It is a sincere heart. This heart expresses truth in all things. People with such hearts have no ulterior motive. They don't conceal anything. Their agendas are always sincere and truthful. People with such hearts become a reflection of God. They have no hidden agenda. Their conscience as the scriptures say is washed with the purest of God's word. The scripture encourages us to draw near to God with this kind of heart because it glorifies the Lord. People with such hearts don't take advantage of God's goodness, they don't come to God because of things or because they want something from God. They are honest in their search for God. They don't hide, cover or defend their shortcomings or weaknesses. They are sincere in telling the Lord they need help. They are not proud of their bad behavior but desire truth change.

Trustful Heart

"Trust in the Lord with all your heart, and lean not on your understanding; In all your ways acknowledge Him, and He shall direct your paths"
(Proverbs 3:5-6;NKJV)

A trustful heart is a heart that has absolute trust in God alone. People with such hearts don't depend on themselves, on anything, or anyone else. They completely trust God for who is and what he promises to do. Their dependence is not on man or their abilities. They don't lean on their own understanding. They are confidently restful in God and believe him for all things. This kind of heart never faints because it trusts the Lord. Individuals with such a heart commit all of their ways to God no matter the size of the problem or situation. They trust God to handle their problems. They are not driven by the problems of life. They don't worry or allow the fear of the unknown to hinder their relationship with the father. They are confidently restful.

LOVING HEART

"So he answered and said,
" 'You shall love the Lord your God with all your heart,
with all your soul, with all your strength, and with all
your mind,' and 'your neighbor as yourself' "
(Luke 10:27;NKJV)

A loving heart is a heart that loves God and all people. People with such hearts love God with all their hearts, might, and soul. They don't hold anything back in loving God. Their love for God will cause them to live a sacrificial life. They are willing to take the risk because of love. They love all people regardless of who they are. They don't choose who to love. For them love is a must for all people. Because of the genuine love, they have for God and others they can easily forgive and give freely to everyone. They are the true reflection of the agape or unconditional love that the Bible wants us to have for everyone. This heart sees as the Lord sees and loves as God loves.

A Caring Heart

"Let each of you look out not only for his interests but also for the interests of others"
(Philippians 2:4;NKJV)

A caring heart is a selfless heart. People with such hearts always look out for others. They are not about themselves. They put people first. They have sincere compassion for everyone. They find so much joy in helping others become better and to succeed in life. They always look out for the poor. They give generously to people without holding back. They are true givers. They always find ways to improve the lives of others. This kind of heart is what God desires to see in all leaders, especially political leaders.

In short, the kind of heart that pleases the Lord and brings him joy is good, pure, God-fearing. Contrite, truthful, trustful, loving, and a caring heart. People with such hearts honor the Lord and these are the hearts that will take us to heaven and help us live under continued open heaven.

CHAPTER THREE
Caring for the Heart

In chapter two I discussed the two categories of heart. The second category of the heart is the heart that pleases the Lord and brings him joy. To maintain and cultivate this kind of heart one has a serious role to play. As I discussed above that God promised to give us a new heart and this heart is the heart that pleases him. When we become saved this heart is given to us spiritually, God removes our old and stoney wrong heart and gives us his heart. In order to maintain this heart, you have to do the following and pay attention to your heart each day. The same way you take care of your health, making sure you eat right and exercise, you do the same with your hearts because this is where the true success of life flows from and your heart will determine where you end up after this life. Is it heaven or hell? I know you desire to be successful and want to spend eternity with God our father. If you do the following, it will help you each day.

Examine your heart daily

"Search me, O God, and know my heart: try me, and know my thoughts; And see if there be any wicked way in me, And lead me in the way everlasting"
(Psalms 139:23-24;ASV)

As you care for your heart daily, examination is a very important part. What is the meaning of examination? EXAMINATION is defined as a detailed inspection or investigation of a thing, situation, or person. It also means to scrutinize, assess, interrogate, test or exam. Searching your heart means assessing all of your thoughts and desires. Are your desires pure? Are they uplifting? Are they wicked? Are they offensive? Are they evil? An honest answer will help you keep a clean heart. If your desires are wicked, impure, evil, and offensive, repent immediately and ask the Lord for mercy. Use the blood of Jesus as your cleansing tool. Most of the time I do this before prayer or before beginning my day. This is something you have to do every day. If your desires and thoughts are pure and uplifting, thank the Lord and ask him for more grace to keep it that way. You can also do this in prayer or whenever you sense you need a heart check.

CHECK YOUR MOTIVES

"Every way of a man *is* right in his own eyes,
but the Lord weighs the hearts"
(Proverbs 21:2;NKJV)

When caring for your heart your motives for doing things have to always be checked. Our reasons for doing things have to be pure and genuine. It has to always come from our hearts, not just mere words or impulses and pressure from people or the world. Why was the reason behind the decision you just made? Why did you sow that seed or offer? Why was the reason behind the phone call you just placed? Why did you marry that person? It is for money or opportunity? Did you truly love that person? Did God tell you to marry that individual? Why are you serving in that church? Is it for the Pastor? Is it for others to know you are doing something for God? What is your motive for joining the choir? Is it to get a husband or wife? Are your daily decisions spirit-led? Are you doing this because of the pressure from people? What is your motive behind every decision and action you take or make? If your answers to these questions are pure and God-driven go ahead and do it. If it is flesh-driven, stop and repent and ask the Lord for help to set your motives right. Pray for a good motive for everything you do. I called this spirit-led motive. Remember the scripture that says" Those who are led by the Spirit of God are the children of God"(Romans 8:14). If **your decisions and actions are led by the precious Holy Spirit you will succeed at whatever you do and the good Lord will always bless the works of your hands and actions of your heart.** Receive that grace now in the name of Jesus.

Pray for a Clean Heart Daily

"Create in me a clean heart, O God,
and renew a right spirit within me"
(Psalms 51:10;ASV).

Caring for your heart requires a daily cleansing. The heart as we have learned is a major part of everything we do, if it stays healthy it will then determine the course of our success in life and making it to heaven. We are to pray daily asking the Lord for a clean heart, the reason is we live in this world where we encounter good and bad circumstances, and sometimes the things that people do to us can easily damage our hearts if we are not careful therefore, asking God for a clean heart each day will help us overcome the storms of life without being bitter toward the situation or the one who has hurt you. The scripture above makes it clear as King David pray and ask the Lord for a clean heart and a right spirit. The History behind Psalm 51 is interesting, this was when David sin against Uriah by committing adultery with Uriah's wife and killing Uriah as a way of cover-up, Nevertheless as we all know nothing can be hidden from God. No amount of cover-up can stop God from seeing our mess and sin. When God showed this to His servant the Prophet Nathan to go and confront David about his wicked actions, David was deeply sorry and realized the sinful condition of his heart led him to his wicked actions, he then began to pray to ask the Lord for a clean heart. The entire story can be found in 2 Samuel 11 & 12. When our hearts are not clean when temptation comes we will fall, so praying daily for a clean heart is one of the ways we care for our hearts.

DON'T HARBOR EVIL IN YOUR HEART

"Do not drag me away with the wicked,
with those who do evil, who speak cordially with their
neighbors, but harbor malice in their hearts"
(Psalm 28:3; NIV).

To keep a clean heart or care for your heart you must avoid carrying malice in your heart towards your neighbor or fellow man no matter what they have done to you. The word harbor according to Merriam Webster is to take shelter, to bear, to cherish, to have, and to hold. When you are harboring evil in your heart, it means you are holding on to evil and cherishing evil in your heart toward someone or a situation and this can lead to you having a bitter heart which can hinder your blessings and relationship with God and others. Do all to avoid sheltering evil or malice in your heart towards anyone.

DON'T DWELL ON EVIL

"Love must be sincere.
Hate what is evil; cling to what is good"
(Romans 12:9;NIV).

Caring for your heart requires you to hate evil at all times. You shouldn't dwell on evil of any kind. This means don't allow evil to reside in your heart. As a believer, you are called to hate evil and cling to what is good. Stay away from evil. Nothing evil pleases God. This is also how you can tell if someone is truly living by the Holy Spirit. As much as God is a God of judgment, he never encourages us to rejoice over evil or wish evil for others. We are to stay blameless by keeping a sincere heart at all times. For example,

If you had a bad experience with someone, avoid dwelling on that incident. If you don't, dwelling on that incident or encounter will increase your chances of developing an evil heart toward that person.

Don't dwell on the bad behaviors of people

The heart is not meant to carry negativity and things that are not of good report. While we are not to encourage the bad behaviors of others, meditating and continuously dwelling on the bad behavior of someone who has done wrong to you can make your heart bitter and can make you create a judgmental attitude towards that person. The bad behavior of that person will control your actions towards them. It will make you a hateful person and malice will settle in your heart and your heart will eventually become unhealthy. In my book "Forgiveness is for you" I describe the different things you can do to overcome hurts and how to live with people who you have forgiven.

One of the things you can do instead of dwelling on the bad behavior or actions of people is to pray and apply Philippians 4:8; NIV" Finally, brothers and sisters, whatever is true, whatever is noble, whatever is right, whatever is pure, whatever is lovely, whatever is admirable if anything is excellent or praiseworthy think about such things" Mediating and praying this scripture will help you set your heart right when the bad actions of people try to invade your precious heart.

DWELL ON GOOD THINGS

"Since then, you have been raised with Christ, set your hearts on things above, where Christ is, seated at the right hand of God. 2 Set your minds on things above, not on earthly things" (Colossians 3:1-2NIV).

Our hearts are special to the Lord and to others. The things we allow can keep it pure and rewarding. As the scripture says above, "set your hearts on things that are above, where Christ is seated" The things that are above are considered pure, godly, good things, and positive things. Whenever you think about heaven, the first thing that comes to mind is joy. In heaven, there is everlasting peace and joy. Nothing evil dwells there. The scripture says where the presence of the Lord is there is fullness of Joy." You make known to me the path of life; you will fill me with joy in your presence, with eternal pleasures at your right hand"(Psalms 16:11 NIV). Occupy your thoughts daily with heavenly things and your heart will dwell on good things.

DWELL ON PURE THOUGHTS

"Let the words of my mouth and the meditation of my heart, be acceptable in Your sight, O Lord, my strength and my Redeemer" (Psalms 19:14;NKJV).

Are your thoughts pure and Holy? Are the things you allow in your heart or minds pure and holy? When caring for our hearts we must do all we can to dwell on pure thoughts. You can't have a pure heart without dwelling on pure things. Let the scripture says let the words of your mouth and the mediation of your heart be acceptable to God. God can only accept what is pure and holy. Remember he is holy and he can only accept a holy heart. God knows it's hard living in this body without wrong thoughts running through your mind and heart. The Lord has given us the grace to choose what to dwell on if we are diligent and sincere with the Lord. Remember we can't do anything by ourselves but with the help of the Holy Spirit, we can dwell on pure and holy thoughts. One of the ways to help you keep a pure thought is to not entertain impure thoughts or allow them to have a hold of your heart. I like this quote from Martin Luther" You cannot keep birds from flying over your head but you can keep them from building a nest in your hair" You can't keep the Devil from suggesting thoughts, but you can choose not to dwell or act on them"[1]. The quote is very true, you have the power by the help of the Holy Spirit to decide what you want to allow in your heart and dwell on. Your ultimate goal is to only allow pure thoughts to abide in your heart each day. Again this has to be done daily during personal prayer time, the start of the day, at the end of the day, or whenever negative thoughts cross your mind take hold of it and pull it down by the power of the blood of Jesus.

---

[1] Rick Warren, *The Purpose Driven Life: What on Earth Am I Here For?*

OWNED YOUR HEART

Owning your heart is very significant to having a pure heart. Do the following and you will own your heart by allowing the Holy Spirit to help you persevere it.

- Don't be controlled by the negativity that occurs around you.

- Don't allow negative people to control your heart.

- Don't pick a fight that is not for you that is if someone is fighting or quarreling with another person don't join the fight,

- Keep a clear conscience and pray for peace.

- Don't allow what someone tells you about another person to make you hate that person.

- Learn to do your research,

- Don't create enemies out of gossip,

- Don't encourage gossip, that is don't entertain gossip, sometimes some people may bring it as a prayer point but be quick to cut it off.

- Don't encourage people around you who have the habit of bad-mouthing their fellow brethren or neighbor.

- Desist from speaking evil of other people. No matter how bad and wicked the person is, the best you can do is to lift a prayer, not gossip.

- Owned your heart by diligently accepting only what is pure, holy, good, godly, and uplifting.

CHAPTER FOUR

Healing of the Hearts
Psalm 34:18

The Lord is near to the brokenhearted
and saves the crushed in spirit.

The Lord wants to heal your heart, the world we live in is filled with evil. The enemy uses people to hurt us. When we are hurt it starts from our heart. The devil knows our hearts matter to God and out of our hearts flow the issues and successes of life, he will therefore do all he can to contaminate our hearts, but I have good news for you. God knows this and has provided an escape and a way out. When you do the following you will experience great healing of your heart no matter what temptation you are faced with and what comes your way your heart will be healed.

COME TO GOD

"Then Jesus said, "Come to me,
all of you who are weary and carry
heavy burdens, and I will give you rest"
(Matthew 11:28; NLT)

When you are hurting due to betrayal or anything that May have caused your heart to be heavy, come to Jesus. Come and he will lift that burden and give you rest. Bring your hurting heart, don't try to fix it on your own. It is impossible, you are wounded and you need tender care, you need the doctor of the heart to help you get healed. The Lord will heal your heart when you come to Him and surrender your pain. When you come to him don't be ashamed to tell him how you feel in your heart towards whoever has hurt you or the situation you are facing. Say it out to the Lord, if even you desire to kill the one that hurt you tell the Lord, he already knows but you saying it out will bring great relief instead of keeping it and becoming bitter. When you come to the Lord and give Him your pain and frustrations he will give you rest and you will be refreshed.

RECEIVE GOD'S REST

*"Take my yoke upon you. Let me teach you,
because I am humble and gentle at heart,
and you will find rest for your souls
Matthew 11:29NLT*

Receiving the rest of God in the process of your heart being healed is very vital. Jesus says in the above scripture he will teach you how to let go because he is humble and gentle at heart, he knows how it feels to be betrayed because he was also betrayed and he wants to teach you how to let go. When you come you must be humble and be willing to learn from the Lord. For instance, the first thing God will ask you to do is to forgive, forgiveness is a very important key in receiving the rest of God. Until you forgive your heart will continue to be heavy. When you forgive you will experience instant relief. So obeying the instructions of God by forgiving your offender is the second step in the healing process.

LEAN ON HIS PROMISES

*"The Lord is close to the brokenhearted;
he rescues those whose spirits are crushed."
Psalms34:18NLT*

Leaning and depending on the promises of God is another important key in the healing of your heart. Almost everything we received in the kingdom of God is the result of faith. Faith is a very essential aspect to receiving from the Lord. Leaning on the promises of God is believing what the scriptures about those who are hurting and broken in their hearts. God promised to be near to those who are heartbroken. The Lord understands the magnitude of the pain you are carrying or dealing with and wants to help rescue you from your pain. Jesus is closer to your heart than that pain, ask him to handle it and tell him you want to be free. He will touch you if you are truly sincere. Receive that grace to lean on the promises of God. The entire Bible is filled with scriptures of healing. Take those scriptures daily and meditate on them and it will help free you from your pain.

CHAPTER FIVE
Rewards of the Hearts

RESULTS OF A WRONG HEART

God is a rewarder and giver of every good gift. Every time he asks us to do something or live a certain way that resembles his character, there is an earthly and heavenly rewarder for our obedience. If we refused to obey or followed his standard for living there are also earthly and eternal consequences for our actions or disobedience. The following are what will happen to people who refuse to care for their hearts.

YOUR UNDERSTANDING IS DARKENED

"Their corrupted logic has been clouded because their hearts are so far from God—their blinded understanding and deep-seated moral darkness keeps them from the knowledge of God
Ephesians4:18TPT

When you have a wrong heart you become darkened in your understanding, This makes you difficult to understand the truth that is the truth of God's word, this was the kind of heart we once had if you are now a believer and this is the heart of unbelievers, that's the reason why the things of God sounds foolish to them due to the hardness of their hearts.

Spiritual Cancer

*"A tranquil heart gives life to the flesh,
but envy makes the bones rot"*
Proverbs 14:30

A wrong heart causes spiritual cancer of the heart, compare what happened to someone with cancer, a person with an envious heart as the scripture says the heart is spiritually rotten. That's the reason why an envious person is always unhappy, resentful, angry, depressed and this person will do everything to destroy their opponents. They are very destructive because their heart is full of negativity.

Unworthy to make heaven

"Take care lest there be an unworthy thought in your heart and you say, 'The seventh year, the year of release is near,' and your eye look grudgingly[a] on your poor brother, and you give him nothing, and he cries to the Lord against you, and you be guilty of sin"
Deuteronomy 15:9

The Lord will consider you unworthy. This means you don't deserve the blessings of God and you are unfit to enter the kingdom of God. This means you will not make it to heaven because heaven will have no place for you. Heaven only receives those who are pure or those who live a holy life. This means Hell will accept you.

Unable to breakthrough

"Listen! The Lord's arm is not too weak to save you, nor is his ear too deaf to hear you call. It's your sins that have cut you off from God. Because of your sins, he has turned away and will not listen anymore."

Most of the time many prayers are not answered because of the condition of the heart. As the scripture says above, God is not the problem and will never be the reason why our prayers are not answered. The problem is the one asking. If your heart is filled with evil and wrong motives you will not receive from the Lord and this will make you unable to breakthrough in life.

People will stay away from you

"The heart is deceitful above all things and desperately sick; who can understand it?

Jeremiah 17:9;EVS

When you have a wicked and wrong heart you will lose good relationships. People will stay away from you. Remember no one wants to be in the company of an evil person. Once your motives and evil desires are revealed others will run from you. The scripture declares above that a deceitful and desperate heart cannot be understood by anyone. People don't know your next action so keeping away is always the best choice because a deceitful person can kill or do anything to get what they want.

Rewards of a Good Heart

YOU WILL SEE GOD

"Blessed are the pure in heart, for they shall see God"
(Matthew 5:8; ESV)

When you have a pure heart you will see God. This means God will hear you when you pray. God will answer you and you will make heaven.

GOD WILL BE GOOD TO YOU

"Truly God is good to Israel,
to those who are pure in heart"
(Psalm 73:1; ESV)

When you have a good heart, God will be good to you in all things. You will experience the goodness of God in your life. The Lord will cause people of all kinds to be good to you. The favor of God will continue to abide with you.

YOU ARE QUALIFIED TO STAND BEFORE GOD

Who shall ascend the hill of the Lord? And who shall stand in his holy place? He who has clean hands and a pure heart, who does not lift his soul to what is false and does not swear deceitfully"
(Psalm 24:3-4; ESV)

A person with a good heart is qualified to stand before God. As the scripture says because your hands are cleansed you will receive from God when you stand before him in prayer, worship and when you call on him he will bless you. A goodhearted person cannot be forsaken.

YOU WILL ATTRACT GOOD PEOPLE

He who loves purity of heart, and whose speech is gracious, will have the king as his friend"
(Proverbs 22:11; ESV)

A person with a good heart will attract good people. God is ever faithful he will bring good people in your path to do business with and to bless you. The king, our Lord, and earthly leaders will befriend you. When you are connected with people in authority due to the kindness of your heart, you will not lack any good things.

You will receive your heart desires

*"Delight yourself in the Lord,
and he will give you the desires of your heart"
(Psalm 37:4; ESV)*

A person with a good heart will receive all of their heart desires. One of the reasons why they receive all of their heart's desire is because their desires will align with God's word. Their desires will also be granted because they are pleasers of God.

Pure Heart and Prayer

Since God is the God of the Heart, that means he sees and judges from the heart, He also answers prayer that truly comes from our hearts. A heartfelt prayer can change any situation. Prayer is very vital to our spiritual life as oxygen to our physical bodies. When one prays with a pure heart he or she touches the heart of God and his or her request will be granted.

Conclusion

Let us draw near with a true heart in full assurance of faith, with our hearts sprinkled clean from an evil conscience and our bodies washed with pure water"
(Hebrews 10:22; ESV)

As I conclude this book I want to let you know that our hearts say it all. It is where all the issues, decisions, and blessings of life flow. Remember a contrite, humble, forgiving, good, and pure heart cannot be forgotten or ignored by God. Most of all a person with a pure heart cannot miss heaven." Strive for peace with everyone, and for the holiness without which no one will see the Lord"(Hebrews 12:14; ESV). Receive a good heart now in the name of Jesus.

www.ingramcontent.com/pod-product-compliance
Lightning Source LLC
LaVergne TN
LVHW020442080526
838202LV00055B/5311